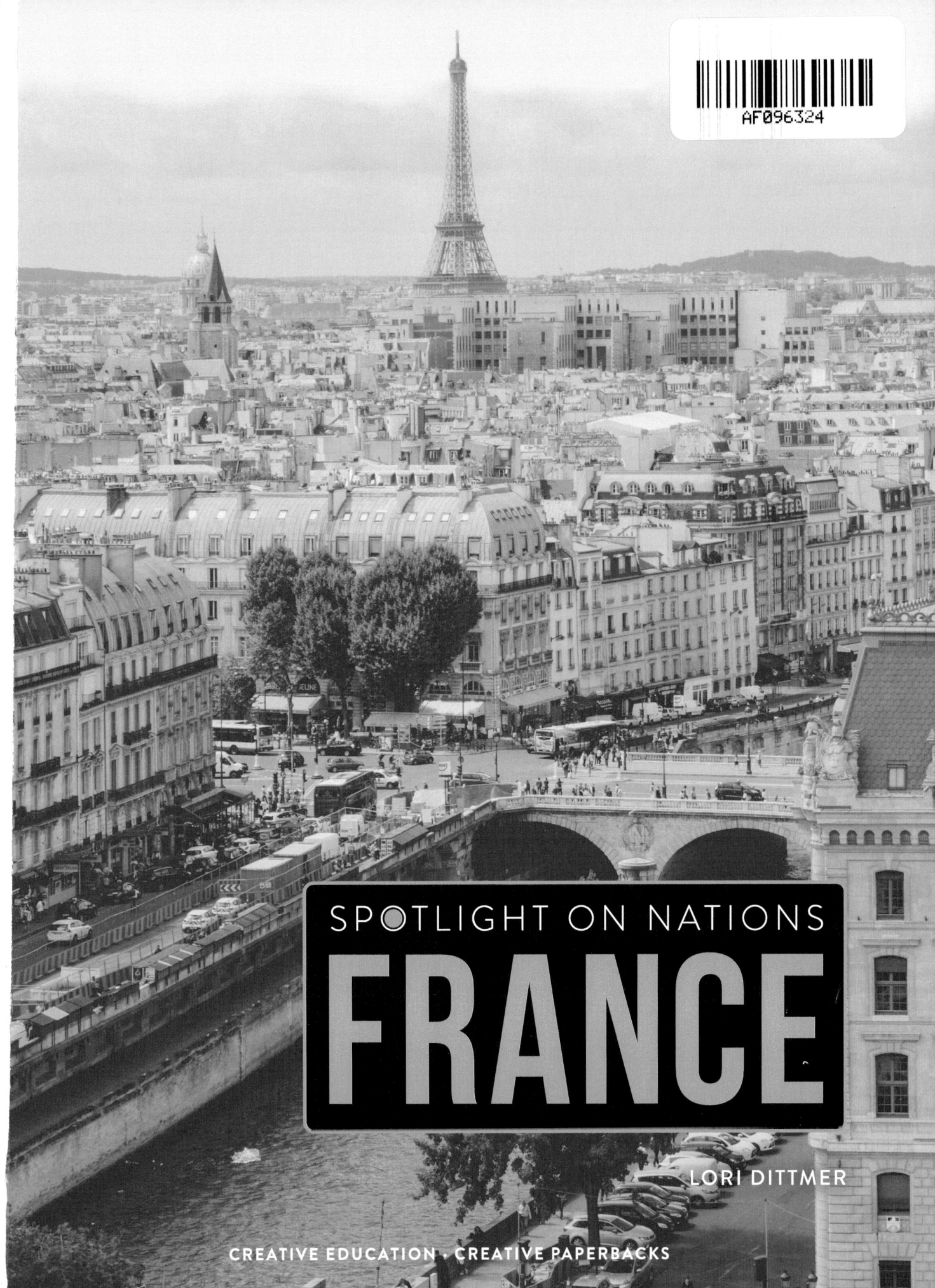

SPOTLIGHT ON NATIONS
FRANCE

LORI DITTMER

CREATIVE EDUCATION • CREATIVE PAPERBACKS

Published by Creative Education and Creative Paperbacks
P.O. Box 227, Mankato, Minnesota 56002
Creative Education and Creative Paperbacks are imprints of The Creative Company
www.thecreativecompany.us

Design and production by Blue Design, Inc.
Art direction by Graham Morgan
Edited by Ana Brauer

Photographs by Getty Images/HUM Images, 10, Tim Bieber, 14, VCG, 23; Pexels/Sebastian Luna, 9; Unsplash/Hongbin, 24, Ilnur Kalimullin, cover, 1, Rob Wingate, 27, Rodrigo Kugnharski, 28; Wikimedia Commons/Andrea Appiani, 6, Claude Monet, 21, Dmitry Makeev, 3, Ermell, 29, Fabien Barrau, 4–5, Jean-Pierre Houël, 12, John Everett Millais, 11, Kremlin.ru, CC BY 4.0, 26, Leonardo da Vinci, 16, Louis-Emile Durandelle, 17, public domain, 8, 10, 14, 16, 18, 20, 22, 27

Every effort has been made to contact copyright holders for material reproduced in this book. Any omissions will be rectified in subsequent printings if notice is given to the publisher.

Copyright © 2026 Creative Education, Creative Paperbacks
International copyright reserved in all countries. No part of this book may be reproduced in any form without written permission from the publisher.

Library of Congress Cataloging-in-Publication Data
Names: Dittmer, Lori author
Title: France / by Lori Dittmer.
Description: Mankato, Minnesota : Creative Education and Creative Paperbacks, [2026] | Series: Spotlight on nations | Includes bibliographical references and index. | Audience: Ages 10–13 | Audience: Grades 4–6 | Summary: "Explore France's history, cultural heritage, notable figures, landmarks, and modern political and economic landscape, plus its global influence and commitment to sustainability. Written for middle-grade readers, this book includes timelines, sidebars, glossary, resources, and index"— Provided by publisher.
Identifiers: LCCN 2025017175 (print) | LCCN 2025017176 (ebook) | ISBN 9798895810705 library binding | ISBN 9798896800231 paperback | ISBN 9798895811962 ebook
Subjects: LCSH: France—Juvenile literature | France—Civilization | France—History | France—Politics and government | France—Description and travel
Classification: LCC DC17 .D55 2026 (print) | LCC DC17 (ebook) | DDC 944—dc23/eng/20250527
LC record available at https://lccn.loc.gov/2025017175
LC ebook record available at https://lccn.loc.gov/2025017176

Printed in the United States

CONTENTS

INTRODUCTION   4
Lighting the Way

A LONG HISTORY   7
A Country of Castles   8
France in World War I   10

THE FIFTH REPUBLIC   13
Notre Dame   14
Choices of Cheeses   16

PEOPLE, CULTURE, AND TRADITIONS   19
Claude Monet (1840–1926)   20
Jules Verne (1828–1905)   22

THE HEXAGON   25
Tour de France   27

All about France   29
Words to Know   30
Learn More   31
Index   32

INTRODUCTION
LIGHTING THE WAY

At 1,083 feet (330 meters) tall, the Eiffel Tower rises above the Paris landscape. This symbol of France is one of the most recognizable structures in the world. Glittering with the sparkle of 20,000 lights, the tower is one reason why Paris is called The City of Light. But there are other reasons. During the 1600s, King Louis XIV (14) wanted to add lights to city streets. A story says he asked people to light candles or oil lamps in their windows at night. Later, Paris became one of the first cities in the world to use gas streetlights. These lights helped people see at night and helped police keep track of criminals. Around the same time, new ideas in **philosophy**, art, and science were spreading. This period was called the Age of Enlightenment. France shone brightly as an example to other countries. Since then, the world has continued to look to France. People are **captivated** by its colorful history, art, and architecture. France leads the way in fashion and food. Politically, it is a major participant in global affairs. Like its glowing past, France continues to be a light in the world.

NAPOLEON BONAPARTE

CLOSE-UP
Emperor Napoleon

Napoleon Bonaparte was a strong military leader in France. In 1799, he took over the government. A few years later, he made himself emperor and became one of the most powerful leaders in Europe.

CHAPTER ONE
A LONG HISTORY

The history of France goes back to ancient times. Long ago, the area was home to many tribes and was called Gaul. By 50 B.C., Rome conquered Gaul. When the Roman Empire fell, a leader named Clovis I took control. He was king of a tribe called the Franks. The land became known as France. Clovis I chose Paris as the capital city. A series of kings and royal **dynasties** followed.

Wars were common. France fought with neighboring countries to gain or protect land. Within the country, noblemen fought each other for power. For centuries, the structure of society was **feudalism**. The nobles made up the upper class and owned land. Peasants lived and worked on the land. They were rarely able to improve their lives.

During the 1500s, Francis I ruled over France. The French Renaissance in art and learning blossomed under his rule. He invited Italian artists to work for him. France sent explorers to the New World and claimed land in the Americas. The idea that each individual person had rights became more popular.

MILESTONES IN FRANCE'S HISTORY

58 B.C.–50 B.C.
- Julius Caesar leads Rome against Gaul in the Gallic Wars. Gaul becomes part of the Roman Empire

481–511 A.D.
- Clovis I unites the Franks. He chooses Paris as the capital city. He is known as the father of France

By the 1700s, life in France was improving. People lived longer. The population doubled. In 1789, France had the largest population in Europe. But the country was deep in debt. The demand for food and goods soared. To raise money, King Louis XVI (16) increased taxes. The lower classes paid the most and had the smallest voice in the government. Angry and frustrated, the people revolted against the monarchy. They started the French **Revolution**. In 1793, King Louis XVI and his wife, Marie Antoinette, were beheaded by the **guillotine**. In 1799, military officer Napoleon Bonaparte took power. He declared himself emperor. He fought to expand French territory. He ruled France until 1815, when he was defeated at the Battle of Waterloo.

CLOSE-UP
Language

If you've ever eaten at a restaurant, enjoyed an *omelette*, read a *novel*, or used an *apostrophe*, you're familiar with French words. All of these came from the French language.

--- HISTORICAL  HIGHLIGHT ---

A Country of Castles

Thousands of castles dot the land of France. The earliest castles were built to keep enemies out. Others were perched on hilltops to give a clear view of approaching invaders. Some were surrounded by moats as another line of defense. Gardens were practical places to grow food. During the 15th century, castles were created as works of art. Ornamental gardens and decorative flourishes were important. One of the most famous castles is the Palace of Versailles. French monarchs lived there in the 17th and 18th centuries.

France faced many struggles, wars, and changes in power. In 1914, as World War I began, France entered the conflict. The Treaty of Versailles, which ended the war, was signed in Paris. During World War II (1938–45), Nazi Germany invaded and took control of France. France was under German control until the end of the war.

From the 1920s to the 1930s, France was one of the largest **colonial** powers. It held claims of land all over the world, including parts of what is now the United States, Canada, and Africa. France also controlled land in the Caribbean and Southeast Asia. Over time, France lost its colonies. The last one was Algeria, Africa. It gained its independence in 1962.

800 A.D.
▸ Charlemagne, also known as Charles the Great, is crowned emperor

MAY 30, 1431
▸ The English burn Joan of Arc at the stake for her role in fighting the Hundred Years' War

CLOSE-UP

Lady Liberty

The Statue of Liberty that stands in the United States today was a gift from France in 1866. It symbolizes freedom and the friendship between the two countries.

— HISTORICAL HIGHLIGHT —

France in World War I

France was one of the main countries that took part in World War I (WWI). It joined Britain and Russia to form the Allied forces. Even before the war, France and Germany had a tense relationship. In the 1870s, France had lost the Franco-Prussian War to Germany. During WWI, many battles took place in northern France. Two of the largest and bloodiest were the Battle of Verdun and the Battle of Somme, both in 1916. Trenches dug through northern France destroyed the countryside. The **economy** of France was hurt. By the end of the war, 1.4 million French people had died.

1431
The English burn Joan of Arc at the stake for her role in fighting the Hundred Years' War.

1516

▸ At the invitation of King Francis I, Italian artist Leonardo da Vinci arrives in France, where he completes his painting of the *Mona Lisa*

1598

▸ King Henry IV (4) issues the Edict of Nantes, which grants religious tolerance to the French protestants

CLOSE-UP
Short Reign

Louis XIX (19) became king after his father, Charles X (10), stepped down during a revolution in 1830. However, Louis quickly decided that he should step down, too. His 20-minute reign is the shortest in world history.

CHAPTER TWO
THE FIFTH REPUBLIC

The people of France embrace the idea of rights for the individual citizen. This is probably why the country has experienced large shifts in its government. During the last 250 years, France has gone through three revolutions. There have been five separate republics. The country has been led by kings, emperors, elected officials, and joint powers. The current government is known as the Fifth Republic. It began in 1959. It is a semi-presidential republic, led by both a president and a prime minister. The people elect the president every five years. This person can serve two terms in office.

The president leads the country's foreign policy. Most of the president's time is spent interacting with other countries. The president also heads the defense system and the French army. The president selects the prime minister. Parliament must agree with this choice. Two houses make up the Parliament. These are the Senate and the National Assembly. The prime minister leads policies in the country. This includes working with Parliament to make or change laws.

1776–83

▸ France supplies the American colonies with money, soldiers, weapons, and ships. This helps the colonies win their independence from Great Britain

JULY 14, 1789

▸ A mob storms the Bastille, a prison used to hold political prisoners. The French Revolution begins

CLOSE-UP
Escargot

Snails, known as escargots, are a popular dish in France. People there eat up to 25,000 tons (22,700 metric tons) per year. This breaks down to about 6.5 snails per person.

——————— HISTORICAL  HIGHLIGHT ———————

Notre Dame

Construction of the Notre Dame Cathedral began in 1163 and ended in 1345. It was built on the remains of two older churches. Notre Dame is known for its two tall towers, which rise 223 feet (68 m) high. Three large, circular windows show stories from the Bible in stained glass. In April 2019, a fire broke out during a renovation project. After five years of repairs and $767 million, the cathedral reopened in 2024. Notre Dame has appeared in several books and movies, including Disney's *The Hunchback of Notre Dame* (1996).

In 2017, the people elected Emmanuel Macron as president. He was re-elected in 2022. In 2024, Macron chose Francois Bayron to be prime minister. He is the sixth prime minister to serve under Macron's presidency.

This government leads France's 18 administrative regions. These are similar to states in the United States. Each one has its own government, but the regions also report to the national government. Thirteen of the regions are in mainland France. The other five are overseas. Four of them are islands: Guadeloupe, Mayotte, Martinique, and La Réunion. The fifth, French Guiana (also called Guyane), is in the northern part of South America.

France is one of 27 members of the European Union (EU). It uses euros, the same currency throughout the EU. France's economy is one of the largest in Europe. It is a major producer of energy. France is one of the world's top nuclear power producers.

Tourism is another large part of the country's economy. Roughly 100 million tourists visited France in 2024. Paris is the most visited city in Europe. People go to see the Eiffel Tower, the Louvre, Notre Dame, and many other historic places. More than 45,000 castles are spread throughout the country. They serve as reminders of France's rich history.

Farming and food processing are other important industries. About one-fourth of the agricultural production comes from fruits, vegetables, and wine. France is famous for its wine, as well as its cheese. France produces 1.7 million tons (1.5 million metric tons) of cheese per year.

JANUARY 21, 1793
- King Louis XVI (16) is put to death by guillotine for trying to convince other countries to invade France to stop the French Revolution

1804
- Napoleon Bonaparte crowns himself Emperor of France

CLOSE-UP
Mona Lisa

The *Mona Lisa*, displayed in the Louvre Museum in Paris, is one of the world's most famous paintings. Each year, it attracts 6 million visitors, some of whom send the painting fan mail.

—— HISTORICAL  HIGHLIGHT ——

Choices of Cheeses

Across the country, farmers raise dairy-producing animals. Much of the milk from cows, goats, and sheep goes to making cheese. After all, France produces as many as 1,000 kinds of cheese. Some are crafted on the farms that produce the milk. Small shops create others. Many varieties come from large manufacturing plants. France is one of the world's leading exporters of cheese. But the people of France are among its biggest consumers. Each person eats about 60 pounds (27 kilograms) of cheese per year. Camembert and brie are French favorites.

1889

The Eiffel Tower opens to the public as part of the International Exposition of 1889.

1860s
› Louis Pasteur develops pasteurization, a heating process that kills microbes and extends the life of foods and beverages

MAY 15, 1889
› The Eiffel Tower opens to the public as part of the International Exposition of 1889

THE FIFTH REPUBLIC

MARIE CURIE

CLOSE-UP
Marie Curie

Marie Curie was born in Poland but did her most important work in France. In 1911, she won the Nobel Prize in Chemistry for discovering radium and polonium. She had already won her first Nobel Prize in 1903 for her work on radioactivity. She was the first person ever to win two Nobel Prizes!

CHAPTER THREE
PEOPLE, CULTURE, AND TRADITIONS

As one of the world's oldest countries, France has a history of diversity and **innovation**. It has been shaped by the groups that invaded it or lived nearby. These include Celtic, Roman, Germanic, and even Viking tribes. Positioned as a bridge between the northern and southern regions of Europe, France's location contributed to its diverse culture. Over the centuries, people passed through the region to trade and work. Many stayed and settled there. The country has also been influenced by its former colonies. These included areas in northern and western Africa, the Caribbean, and Southeast Asia.

More than half of the French population identify as Roman Catholic. Another quarter of the population say they are nonreligious. More recently, **immigration** has helped grow the country's Muslim population. France has one of the largest Muslim populations in Europe, at about 5 million.

The French have a tradition of taking time to savor meals while socializing with friends and family. Dinners often feature several courses. People enjoy

1907
- Architect Eugene Henard designs one of the first roundabouts. Twelve lanes circle around the landmark Arc de Triomphe in Paris

1919
- The Treaty of Versailles is signed, ending World War I and redrawing European borders

their meals for hours at a time. Even during the workday, people take time for long lunches and coffee breaks at outdoor cafes.

French innovation has led to many iconic dishes. Ratatouille is a comforting vegetable stew. Quiche Lorraine is a pie made from cream, eggs, bacon, and cheese. Crêpes are thin pancakes served folded around fillings.

French creativity has led to other innovations, too. The hot air balloon and the parachute were both developed during the late 1700s. The first film camera was created in France. Soon after, French innovators made moving pictures. The 1902 film *Le Voyage Dans la Lune (A Trip to the Moon)* was the first science fiction film. It shows a space capsule landing on the Moon. Filmmaker Georges Méliès was inspired by the writings of French author Jules Verne.

HISTORICAL HIGHLIGHT

Claude Monet (1840–1926)

Claude Monet sold his first piece of art at 15 years old. At the time, he was drawing caricatures of people. Later, he became known as a leader in the Impressionist movement. His work usually featured scenes from everyday life and nature. He often painted the same subject at different times of day, capturing how the light changed. Some of his famous works focused on stacks of hay and water lilies. After he died, his work became even more popular. Today, Monet's paintings are displayed in museums around the world.

WOMAN WITH A PARASOL, CLAUDE MONET (1875)

1940
- The Franco-German Armistice reflects France's surrender to Germany during World War II

2002
- France adopts the euro as its currency, replacing the franc

PEOPLE, CULTURE, AND TRADITIONS

There are many celebrations in France. Many are tied to past innovations. The Cannes Film Festival takes place each year and showcases European films. It is one of the most famous film festivals in the world. Another event is the Grand Est Mondial Air Balloons festival. Hundreds of hot air balloons fill the sky during the 10-day event. The event honors the history of balloon flight. France also celebrates Bastille Day each year on July 14. It marks the country's freedom from monarchy. It is celebrated with fireworks and parades.

CLOSE-UP
Mont Blanc

The French Alps are part of a large chain of mountains. The highest point is Mont Blanc, which sits on the border of France and Italy. At 15,771 feet (4,807 m), it is the tallest mountain in Western Europe.

HISTORICAL HIGHLIGHT

Jules Verne (1828–1905)

Jules Verne often wrote about innovations that did not yet exist. This made him one of the earliest science fiction writers. He grew up in Nantes, a busy port city. He watched the coming and going of ships. This inspired his ideas of adventure for his stories. Many are considered classics and are still popular today. *Twenty Thousand Leagues Under the Sea* is an ocean adventure. *Journey to the Center of the Earth* drills down through the ground. *Around the World in Eighty Days* takes its characters on a global quest.

2024
Summer Olympics are held in Paris.

2019
▸ A fire in the Notre Dame cathedral damages a large portion of the building

2024
▸ Summer Olympics are held in Paris. Athletes from 206 countries take part in 329 medal events

CHAPTER FOUR
THE HEXAGON

France covers roughly the same area as the state of Texas. The country shares its borders with a variety of bodies of water and many neighbors, including Germany, Switzerland, and Spain. On a map, France has the general appearance of a six-sided polygon, so the French refer to their nation as *L'Hexagone* (the Hexagon). France is the third-largest country in Europe. It also contains a variety of landscapes, from the snow-covered peaks of the French Alps to the rolling hills of the countryside. The French Riviera, located along the coast of the Mediterranean Sea, is a famous luxury resort area known for its beaches.

A modern nation, France is a global power. It is a member of several international organizations, including the European Union (EU), the United Nations (UN), **NATO**, and the G7. France has adopted a plan to protect its waterways and coastlines from changing climate patterns. It is working toward using **sustainable** farming methods. It has set the goal to reduce its emission of greenhouse gases.

France has an efficient system of public transportation. The TGV (Train à Grande Vitesse) is a high-speed train. It goes as fast as 200 miles (320 kilometers) per hour! It connects cities throughout France and into other countries. Buses, trams, and metro lines carry people to their destinations.

CLOSE-UP
Champions

Soccer is one of France's most popular sports. The national team, *Les Bleus* (The Blues), won the World Cup in 1998 and 2018. Both wins brought pride and celebrations across the country.

The world looks to France for inspiration in fashion and art. Since 1973, Paris Fashion Week has thrilled fans twice a year with the latest clothing styles from the top designers. More than 1,000 museums showcase European art and history. The most famous one is the Louvre. It is home to Leonardo da Vinci's **Mona Lisa** and Claude Monet's **Haystacks**.

Major sporting events are hosted in France. The French Open is an international tennis tournament held in Paris. It is one of four Grand Slam events, with the others played in the U.S., Australia, and England. The Tour de France is a challenging and famous bicycle race. Fans and participants flock to the country every July. The world's oldest motor car race is held in Le Mans each year, where teams of racers drive for 24 hours straight. In 2024, Paris hosted the Summer Olympic Games. It marked 100 years since the last time Paris had hosted the summer games.

Since its beginning, France has been a central part of the world. Today, the Hexagon continues to set trends in fashion, art, and science. It attracts attention through its innovative and independent spirit.

── HISTORICAL  HIGHLIGHTS ──

Tour de France

The first Tour de France was held in 1903. People hoped it would boost sales of a magazine. Since then, it has become an international event. The race takes place over 23 days. Each day has a route, called a stage. Each stage has a winner. The overall winner is the racer with lowest time over all stages. Teams have several riders. Team members work together to support the rider who has the best chance of winning. The route changes each year, but the race always ends in Paris.

ALL ABOUT
FRANCE

Continent: Europe

Capital city: Paris

Population size: 66.6 million

Main language spoken: French

Type of government: Semi-presidential republic

Currency: Euro

Main religions practiced: Roman Catholicism, Muslim

Colors on flag: Blue, white, red

National flower: Iris, also known as the fleur-de-lis

WORDS to Know

captivate — to attract and hold the interest of someone

colonial — controlled by one power over a dependent area or people

dynasty — a line of rulers from the same family over a long period

economy — the wealth and resources of a country

feudalism — a political system in the Middle Ages in which people gave kings and lords money in exchange for protection

guillotine — a machine used for cutting off a person's head

immigration — the action of coming to live in a foreign country

innovation — coming up with new ideas for products and ways of doing things

NATO — North Atlantic Treaty Organization, a group of countries from Europe and North America that work together to keep its members safe

philosophy — the study of basic ideas about right and wrong and the meaning of life

revolution — a forcible overthrow of government

sustainable — a method of using a resource in a way that the resource is not depleted

LEARN MORE

Books

Loh-Hagan, Virginia. *The French Revolution.* Ann Arbor, Mich.: Cherry Lake Publishing, 2021.

Re, Laura, and Celli, Daniela. *Around Paris.* New York: White Star Kids, 2023.

Van, R.L. *France.* Minneapolis, MN: Abdo, 2023.

Websites

"France Facts." National Geographic Kids.

https://www.natgeokids.com/uk/discover/geography/countries/facts-about-france/

"France Facts: Interesting Facts for Kids." Kids World Travel Guide.

https://www.kids-world-travel-guide.com/france-facts.html

"The French Revolution." Crash Course European History. https://www.youtube.com/watch?v=I5fJl_ZX9iIo

Documentaries

Rubenstein, David, host. *Iconic America: The Statue of Liberty.* PBS, 2023.

Villemiont, Florence, and Genie Godula, hosts. *French Connections - for the Love of Food!* FRANCE 24, May 31 2019.

Worsley, Lucy, host. *Marie Antoinette: The Doomed Queen.* PBS, 2020.

Note: Every effort has been made to ensure that any websites listed above were active at the time of publication. However, because of the nature of the Internet, it is impossible to guarantee that these sites will remain active indefinitely or that their contents will not be altered.

Visit

CAVE PAINTINGS AT LASCAUX

Step into a replica of the famous cave to view reproductions of prehistoric drawings made thousands of years ago.
Avenue de Lascaux, 24290 Montignac, France

COLIN DU CHÂTEAU

Explore panoramic views of Nice from this historic hilltop park, featuring lush greenery, waterfalls, and remains of an ancient castle.
Rue des Ponchettes, 06300 Nice, France

LOUVRE

Walk through the most visited museum in the world and view famous works of art, including the Mona Lisa.
Rue de Rivoli 99, 75001 Paris, France

MONT SAINT-MICHEL

Tour the abbey that was built on top of a large rock formation and used as a fortress during the Middle Ages.
Grand Rue, 50170 Le Mont-Saint-Michel, France

INDEX

Bonaparte, Napoleon, 6, 8, 15
Clovis I, 7
colonies, 9, 13, 19
Curie, Marie, 18
Eiffel Tower, 4, 15, 17
Fifth Republic, 13
governments, 8, 13, 15
Hexagon, 25, 26
innovations, 19, 20, 22, 26
Louvre, 15, 16, 26
Macron, Emmanuel, 15

Mona Lisa, 11, 16, 26
Monet, Claude, 20, 26
Notre Dame, 14, 15, 23
Olympics, 23, 26
Paris, 4, 7, 9, 15, 16, 19, 23, 26, 27
revolutions, 8, 12, 13, 15
Tour de France, 26, 27
transportation, 25
Verne, Jules, 20, 22
World War I (WWI), 9, 10, 19